Always Rem[ember]
when you "SHIFT"
new possibilities are
created!

~Michelle

Shifting Experiences

What an eye-opener! Smith's book reads almost like a guidebook to your future, and you'll want to share this new found and insightful information with everyone you know. Her helpful hints, tips and strategies can be used towards any aspect of life and encourages us to take that leap of faith without fear. In each chapter, the author flawlessly explains the similarity between chameleons and human beings' need for change and a new outlook. Our spirit is constantly altering, and the process of a healthy growth begins with us taking the first step. The concepts explained by her superb writing talent are easy to follow and can be practiced on a daily basis in order to achieve complete serenity within yourself in no time at all. A must-read for those truly looking for a new start to a new you!

—JAIMIE GERALDI, *Freelance Writer*

Smith's promise to share her grandmother's wisdom to the world in a unique way is just enough to capture readers' attention. As one progresses through this thought-provoking book, they may find themselves nodding their heads in agreement or taking notes in the margin. I really enjoyed the author's bold confessions of her own past which helped me to understand her point entirely. And, her special gift of explaining things thoroughly is just an added bonus. This book could save your life and prove beneficial in the long run whether you're searching for love, trying to improve your work ethic or just attempting to be a better person. Highly entertaining, powerful at times and a clever way to convince people that it's never too late to be the person you want to be; just shift! And, I even learned some unknown facts about chameleons that I never knew!

—MICHELLE CASTILLO, *Article Write Up*

THE INVISIBLE
CHAMELEON

Changing Your Color, Shifting and Reaching A Desired Goal

Michelle A. Smith

*This book is dedicated
to my loving grandmother, Imogene Miller.
This is my promise to share your wisdom
with the world.*

Acknowledgements

To my Creator, I give my deepest appreciation,
gratitude and submission for your abundant favor
bestowed upon me.
You are the only one worthy of worship.

Contents

INTRODUCTION

When thinking about what the missing piece is, the gap between wanting something so bad and getting what you want, there is one thing that stops us all...dead in our tracks. It takes up the space of matter and time that leaves us thinking, wanting, and yearning to just get there, to grab it, hold it, to conquer it! If only we could just transform into that thing, and become that person, so we could just perform the action necessary to get what we want. If only we could just fill in that space, that gap called FEAR!

When I think about my life and how many times fear has stopped, startled, confused, bewildered and just plain ol' scared me out of doing something, including writing this book, I realized how many more times I overcame this disease. You see what has worked for me and continues to prove itself over and over is my ability to change, adapt, be flexible and to shift, right there in the moment (impromptu sometimes), without notice or warning, when fear steps right in front of me.

I believe it is a gift that I didn't know I had until this gift surprisingly and often unaware just shows up, just when I need it to. This gift is like the qualities of a chameleon lizard; it changes color within a blink of an eye and adapts to whatever environment it is in.

As life continues to happen for me and to me, I have built quite a toolbox of chameleon characteristics. I pull from this box daily in order to face my fears and grab hold of the things I desire most. Primarily, it gives me the ability to discern which characteristics I need in order to get the outcome I want.

The Invisible Chameleon is an analogy, an oxymoron of sorts, which describes how the blending in and standing out survival tactics helps me. This book will show that you can change your external color and shift without changing who you are on the inside - your core. It is a tool to help you get past the gap, over the hurdle, through the space, and reach your desired outcome.

I hope, wish and pray that after reading this book in its entirety that I have provoked thought and provided you with a powerful leverage to use in your life.

SECTION I

The Chameleon

1

Color Changing

FACT: Did you know chameleons can change colors in as quick as 20 seconds - from brown to green and black and more? Special pigment cells called chromatophores, allow them to go through a metamorphosis of sorts.

Did you know you too can go through a metamorphosis almost as quick? It's as simple as a mind shift.

Many people think chameleons change color to blend in with their surroundings. Some scientists disagree. Studies show that light, temperature and even mood can cause this color shift. Sometimes changing color can make the chameleon more comfortable and other times it helps the animal communicate with other chameleons.

As I look back on my life and even my everyday comings and goings, I realize how essential it is to be able to change your color, especially when your mood controls how your day will be. How many times have you woken up to a dreary, rainy day and it sets your mood for the rest of the day? Besides not wanting to leave your cozy bed to go to work or school, you find yourself saying, "this is a stay in, watch a movie and eat junk kind of day!" Just like that, within a matter of seconds the temperature, lack of light or sunshine has altered your mood. Then within a minute, despite the weather outside, you created a better scenario of what you would "rather" do, and that scenario would make you happy. What if you were able to create scenarios, or use mechanisms that could help alter your mood, temporarily, so you could get the desired outcome you wish? Let's break this down even further.

In a matter of 20 seconds Chameleons can change from brown to green and back. I remember a specific Monday morning, May 2007, I was one week into my new job as an Investment Banking Recruiter and also two days fresh into my breakup with my boyfriend (and the man I thought was "The One") of two years. Random and impromptu, the breakup call was nothing more than, "I can't do this anymore, I don't want to be with you anymore and that's it!" I was left on the other end of the phone devastated, confused, hurt, sad, and confused some more and totally caught off guard. I cried until I had a headache, no appetite, and the pain of the heart break just made me feel weak in the knees. Yet, I had just started a new job, of which I had to engage and interact with people all day. I needed to be cheery, pleasant and pretty much a walking advertisement of this new company, to attract top talent. However, I woke up that morning and barely wanted to get out of bed, comb my hair, and get dressed much less put a smile on my face and talk to people. To make matters worse, this awesome new job that I was so excited about came about because of a recommendation of my best friend, who I just could not let down nor disappoint. We were gearing up for one of the biggest recruiting events the bank has ever had. I had to be on point - on top of my game, flexible, quick thinking, and be able to manage an invite list of over 200 people, including the CEO of the company.

Unfortunately, on this Monday morning my color was dark, grey, mixed with black and blue. I coached myself enough to get dressed, look semi decent, get on the train, and make it to the office without crying. I made it up to my office, closed the door and fell apart. Then I remembered one of the best pieces of advice I received early in my career and that was *"If you have to cry, go outside!"* In the world called Wall Street, there was no room for tears, frowns or even feelings. You have to appear somewhat immortal. No one cared about your problems, how you were feeling, or showed sympathy. It was code that you never let anyone see you sweat. I say that with the caveat that people break down all the time, it just happened to be when no one was watching. I knew I couldn't let anyone see me like that, especially being 'the new kid on the block.' I went into the restroom and I stared at myself in the mirror, red, puffy eyes and all. I said to myself *"Michelle, pull yourself together. Put on your game face and get this done. You can cry later!"* I knew deep down inside I had to change my attitude, my mood, my color and I had to do it quickly before anyone else came in the office. So just like that I convinced myself (pretty much tricked myself) that in order to appear happy (at least to make it through that day and evening), I had to think good thoughts, about anything that made me happy. I had to be confident, friendly, inviting and open in order to pull this event off. I also knew this job was a big step in my career and it had to be successful. I reminded myself that feelings and emotions are just temporary. For instance, one minute you could feel hungry then 30 minutes later after eating a steak dinner, you could feel tired. Your feelings and your emotions are all variables, not a constant. You may not have control over a situation, however you DO have control over how you react to it. You have to want a better outcome, or to reach your goal so badly that it overpowers the feelings that are making you weak and distracted.

So here I am in the restroom; disheveled, disoriented, not present and simply just suffering from broken heart syndrome. I knew that speaking to him, getting answers, or just simply hearing his voice would have made me feel so much better, but that wasn't going to happen. Nor could I stop my day, my work, my responsibilities or my life because someone made a decision to walk away from me. I loved this new job and I wanted to succeed in it more than anything.

So for those moments, seconds, minutes and hours, although my light was dim and my mood somber, *I chose to make a shift.* I knew that once I got home, I would have an opportunity to mourn the end of my relationship, so I wanted to use the current time wisely and be productive. I washed my faced, fixed my hair, fixed my posture and walked out of the bathroom to face my Monday.

Chamo Chapter Tip

SHIFT...
it does a
body good!

2

Well-rounded Vision

FACT: Did you know that chameleons possess 360 degree arc of vision and can actually focus on two different things in opposite directions at the same time? Even with pinhole size openings for the pupil to peer through, they can spot prey with the sharpest stereoscopic vision and depth! It's kind of like a super power and a huge leverage for the little guys!

Wow! What would life be like if we could have a 360 degree field view of things? Likely we would have made different decisions and choices. Perhaps, we would have moved forward with things we were once apprehensive of. Consequently, where we are right now could have been a totally different scenario had we viewed things with a wider lens.

What if I told you that if you wanted, figuratively, you too could be like the chameleon and have 360 degree arc of vision? Scientists have proven that the chameleon can rotate and focus separately to observe two objects at the opposite ends of the spectrum simultaneously. This concept is usually not the most practical as most people are taught to focus on just one thing at a time. While in some cases that holds true; I believe that it is okay to have your eyes set on more than one thing at a given time. My reasoning for this is because what happens if that one thing does not work out or yields in your favor? Do you just stop and search for the next thing, or do you move forward with the alternatives you have had brewing in the background?

Having tunnel vision is probably the most disciplined challenging quality one could have.

It means that's you have your eye fixated on one thing and no matter what, you are not looking at any distractions to the left or right of you. Tunnel vision is like looking out of your windshield, driving straight and not having a rearview mirror. You have no concerns to look back, for what? What you want is straight ahead of you. The rewards of having tunnel vision are awesome. It reduces time and you achieve your goal much quicker. However, tunnel vision is a very selfish mission and can only be travelled with one person, yourself! You have to block out everyone and everything in your peripheral and often times that means sacrificing, time spent with others, enjoying activities, and even sleep. Tunnel vision is a great quality to have yet realistically, most people are not strong enough to focus on just one thing. I, for one, lack this quality and probably would have finished this book a lot sooner.

Having 360 degree vision is an ability that still requires focus, but be able to monitor other factors going on around you. 360 degree vision equates to multi-tasking. For example, most people have a job or a career that they work for every day. That job   allows the opportunity to support yourself, provide for yourself and your family, have a home, food on your table and cover your bare necessities. Some people enjoy   their job or profession so much that they work until they retire from that organization. There are others that desire to own their own company   or even have an additional source of income aside from their salary. Without even knowing, the ability to work on simultaneous businesses requires having 360 degree vision. Working a 9 to 5 job is taxing in itself and typically drains you of all your attention. With only 24 hours in a day, being successful in your day to day job and devoting your time into another passion, or even an activity, growing your talents can only be accomplished with this type of vision. It also takes discipline to focus on two things at once.   Let's be honest, as humans we can get distracted very quickly and lose focus on either object at the same time.

Well-rounded vision also leads to seeing the glass half full. With every negative in your life, there should be at least one positive you can pull from it. Have you ever been in a car accident? While the car may be damaged, with a glass half full perspective you understand the car can be fixed or replaced and at least you're alive to see either happen.

Having well-rounded vision can also mean seeing perspective in a setback. Have you ever been rejected or declined, for a particular job, a position? Perhaps it is something you wanted really badly and the response was just "No!" As hard as it may seem, sometimes you have to take a step back as a set up for your next step. Every "no" you have ever received is one step closer to your "yes". I have recognized a pattern that every time something doesn't work out in my favor; it was a precursor for something better to happen at a different time. A Shift Up!

Chamo Chapter Tip

"Having 360 degree vision is an ability that still requires focus, but be able to monitor other factors going on around you."

3

Happy Feet

FACT: Did you know that the chameleons feet are adapted to grasp small to large objects of all shapes, sizes and surfaces to hang on for dear life? They have five toes grouped in a flattened section of either two or three toes which make them appear tong-like. The front and rear feet are reversed in their structure giving them the ability to be dexterous, so no matter which way they have to hang, they are good to go!

Who knew that chameleons had five toes just like us! While their toes separate like tongs or the Star Trek Vulcan salute, it has one distinct action, to grip tightly onto narrow surfaces. While you don't realize it, we too use our toes to not only walk but to grip onto surfaces some narrow, rocky, smooth, slippery and uphill.

Remember in chapter one I talked about life throwing curveballs that we are not always prepared for? Well, sometimes your environment can be a variable as well and you may not always be standing on a smooth surface, walking or running like a gazelle through the fields. There are times where you may lose your footing because the ground or your foundation is not stable, causing you to slip and fall.

In 2008, just like the market, my world came crashing down. Here I was focused and knee deep into my career and then the pink slip was handed to me. This was the first time I had ever been laid off and the first time since I was 14 years old that I went without a job. To make matters worse, the job market was what I called "the crab in a barrel market." Half of Wall Street was unemployed and everyone was just clawing on top of each other just to find a job to provide for their families and make ends meet. I admit I too was a crab. The career that I was on the fast track for and sacrificed hours of my personal life was just ripped away from me. Just like that, my young New York lifestyle went along with it. My foundation - my entire structure was a moving target - rocky, shaky and very unstable.

Usually when your life is turned upside down and you feel like the floor is dissolving right under your feet you start to grab hold to anything you can find and hold on for dear life. Isn't it ironic the chameleon does the same thing?

I was clawing my way around the job market barrel and I realized the only thing that changed was someone bigger than me pushing me further down. I had to do something different; I had to make a move and so I did, literally, and landed in Houston, TX.

I moved to Houston with no friends or family. I literally packed up all my belongings and did like the birds and headed south. About 80% of my family and friends thought I was losing my mind to leave everything I have ever known, my security blanket, and go to a place where I would be the cheese that stood alone. The other 20% of my support system was just that, rooting for me and secretly wanting to see how I was going to do it. You see, what no one knew was my desire to succeed and make a comfortable life for myself was just as strong as me needing air to breathe.

I couldn't wait around to temporarily seal the cracks in my foundation. It was almost like a crack in a windshield that starts off small and within minutes spreads three feet wide.   I was desperate to plant my feet on solid ground again and by any means necessary I was going to do that.

Moving to Texas was the best decision I ever made in life. Not only am I doing twice as better than I was in New York, but I made and built bonds with people that I know will last for a lifetime. The opportunities here are endless and I seem to be in the right place at the right time quite frequently.

In sharing this part of the journey, I want to point out that change does not come without trials. The transition to this new territory, solo, was not easy and I had many days of doubt. At one point, I almost convinced myself that I had made a major mistake in thinking I could start over somewhere else and walk on solid ground again.

There were things that did not go according to plan once I moved here. Actually, everything that could possibly go wrong, did! Just when I got to the point of defeat, ready to throw my hands up and just turn around and move back to the place I was most familiar with, the cracks in my foundation were sealed. I didn't have to cling or hold onto anything to keep from falling. I used my toes as the chameleon did and rebuilt a new network that to this day was the most instrumental factor in me staying in Houston.

When your foundation seems like sinking sand, don't just give in. Use ambition, drive, and the desire to succeed as your toes and you grab hold to your vision. Remember at some point you will regain your footing and you will plant your feet on solid ground again.

Chamo Chapter Tip

"When your foundation seems like sinking sand, don't just give in. Use ambition, drive, and the desire to succeed as your toes and grab hold of your vision."

4

You Are What You Speak

FACT: Did you know that the chameleons tongue is one and a half to twice as long as the entire length of their body? Talk about a long tongue! Chameleons project that bad boy out like a bullet to capture their prey with the accuracy of a marksman and in the speed of light! Well not really the speed of light but, in as little as 0.07 seconds! Now that is a powerful tongue in a very little body!

I do believe there is power in the tongue. I believe that things we constantly repeat will manifest itself in some way, shape or form. I believe that words are sometimes sharper than action and can have a major effect on you and those around you.

If I got a dollar for every time I heard the phrase, "Speak life into it!" or "Speak it into existence" I would be a millionaire by now. Self-consciously we speak life into things just about every time we open our mouths.

Not only is a chameleon's tongue long and powerful, it is also very quick catching their prey often times totally off guard! Figuratively, we as humans have that same characteristic.

When meeting or speaking with someone, not only are we first judged on our appearance, we are also judged by what we say. Your words in conversation are connectors between you and an individual. Mostly we think about what we are about to say before we allow it to roll off our tongue and leave our mouth. We take a few seconds to formulate the words to convey what our brain wants to say. Yet, there are many times we speak so quickly without thought that it can often result in an adverse outcomes. I am guilty as charged for doing both.

Our tongues are just as commanding as the chameleons. What we say can project to far distances and capture another person's attention, change the dynamic of an environment, and evoke emotion. The speed in what we say can travel and resonate very quickly. We are what we speak. Society says that communication is the key to success and I believe knowing how to communicate is even more important.

In this chapter, I want to help you identify your inner voice; after all, what's inside you is what you project to the rest of the world. Going back to chapter one, I mentioned going through a very depressing time in my life where I had to self-coach myself in the ladies room just to get through my day. That was one example of how powerful your words are, that even in the bleakest of situations you can talk yourself off the ledge and to a point of functioning as normal as possible.

How about a more relatable situation? Ever

have a moment at work or school, and there is one person who seems to just ride on that very last nerve you have? The sound of their voice irritates you to no end. You create a very vivid scene in your mind where you creatively silence them - removing them from your presence. Yes, we have all been there. One day I decided to try something different. I came up with a new communication strategy.

What I realized were two things: I was letting this person get to me, allowing them to get under my skin and I was showing them this through my demeanor. Remember, with every action, there is a reaction. So in changing my action of the way I communicated to this individual, it would yield a different reaction from them. I chose to communicate in a manner that was more positive, uplifting, and just overall more pleasant. Was I being fake? Absolutely not! Let's be clear, I did not go overboard nor was I extending invites for Sunday dinners. What I was simply doing was communicating my inner peace and joy through my demeanor and not allowing their negative factors to penetrate that.

It appeared to me that the more pleasant I spoke, the more irritated and annoyed they became. There was a point where I thought this individual was trying to call my bluff or see how long I could keep this "friendly" persona up. Much to their surprise, I never stopped.

As time went on, I had an "ah ha" moment and a few things became clear to me:

1. If an individual was unhappy in their personal lives, they will more than likely carry it over into other areas, especially their professional lives.

2. You have a choice to inherit someone's negative attitude, allowing them to affect your mood.

3. At some point, whether they will ever admit it or not, your communication style will affect them in some way, shape or form.

Again, you are what you speak. Your words have super powers that can control your actions and the actions of others.

Like the chameleon using their tongues to catch their prey, use your tongue to form words that make an impact; not only for yourself, but for others as well.

Chamo Chapter Tip

"You are what you speak!"

5

The Anti-Social

FACT: Did you know that chameleons are introverts and tremendously territorial to the extreme that they even snub other chameleons? Let alone, when another enters their domain it turns in to a shape shifting amazing performance of puffed body, aggressive dance, jaw clacking, whistling, and a display of lights in a sense with the menacing color changing show! The loser of such a battle will leave with its tail between its legs adapting to the defeated color of a pale-gray.

It surprised me that the chameleon likes to stay in its comfort zone and roll solo. Sound like anyone you know?

No one knows you better than yourself. It is because of this that you can rely on your own internal intuition; that personal judgment that allows you to make decisions every day. If you're anything like me, I have fun by myself. I love living in my own world, because I am most understood there. That solitary space is free of judgment, ridicule, perceptions, or opinions. It allows you to take off any masks that you use to cover up fears and insecurities. Solitude equals freedom. Or so we often believe.

Surely in any space that one can be free, you want to keep it out of harm's way, protect it, and secure it from anyone who tries to enter. You become territorial and can have an arsenal of defense weapons ready to use should anyone try to enter.

I, for one, thrive in a solitary space. I am actually more confident being solo than being with a team. For a long time I thought it was ok to be this way. I didn't have anyone to double check me on anything, call me out on anything, point out my flaws, or just simply have to answer to anyone. Over the past few years, from sheer life experiences I realize that being in a solitary space actually holds you back.

First, let me say this, in all things find balance. Having alone time, being centered with your own thoughts and feelings, or just simply taking a moment for yourself away from the rigmarole of life is always a good thing to do. However, allowing being solitary as a priority can hinder you. It stunts your creativity, blocks you from opportunity, tricks you into thinking it's comfortable, and that being comfortable is ok. It's not!

No matter where you are in life, what you do for a living, or what your age is, settling for comfort is the fastest way in becoming President of the Lazy Association. Now, I don't want you to take the word "comfort" and confuse it with the act of being "comfortable." I have a good job, I live a fairly good life, and I am in good health, which for me is comfort. However, my goals, my dreams, and my ambition to want and do more for myself do not allow me to be comfortable with my current situation. When you're comfortable you become territorial, because you are trying to protect your safe space. As I continuously talk about the variables of life throughout this book, those same variables can most certainly infiltrate that barrier you have around your comfort territory and change the environment within seconds.

This has happened to me several times, where the rug was pulled out from under my comfortable space and I was left confused, empty, and without direction. After so many curveballs knocking down the walls of my comfort space, I decided something had to give. Moving halfway across the country, by myself, was the biggest step out of my comfort zone ever!

I developed a habit of doing things that were UNCOMFORTABLE to me. That meant thinking outside of the box, always forward thinking, being one step ahead while having three more chess moves in my back pocket. Trust me when I tell you there is nothing fun about doing things that are uncomfortable. What I can tell you though is when it feels uncomfortable it is a clear indication you are heading in the right direction.

Think about this example: You want to shed a few pounds. You have a desired weight in mind, a dress you want to sport, or, to look amazing on the beach with toned muscles. Guess what? That requires you to start eating right and ditch your favorite junk foods, going to the gym, and working out consistently and frequently. I could count on one hand how many people would consider that comfortable. However, being uncomfortable actually gets you to the results you so desperately want.

...

I found out a few cool things when you step outside of your comfort zone:

1. You tend to meet people who are also in an uncomfortable space similar to yours and become "Comfortably Uncomfortable Buddies." You then gain a network of others that support you and swap coping mechanisms during this phase.

2. Opportunities start popping up all around you. There will be opportunities that you would have never imagined that will present themselves.

3. Once you successfully master one uncomfortable space, the next one you enter becomes surprisingly easier to navigate.

4. You start to build a toolbox of lessons learned: things that worked and didn't work, and best practices and remedies that make the process smoother to maneuver through.

5. Your recovery time gets quicker if you fall short (and there will be times that you will fall short). You learn to brush off your knees and keep on going.

6. You become the "Uncomfortable Space Spokesperson" and you start to influence those around you with your actions. You start to spark their curiosity to also want to take a step out of their Comfort Land and see what adventure awaits them.

7. There will be no need to be territorial because there will be no comfortable space to protect.

8. Like most things it is only temporary. Short term pain for long term pleasure.

I couldn't imagine where I would be today if I had stayed in the spot that was warm and fuzzy. I surely would not have travelled the world, have the opportunity to meet some of the most amazing people, and participate in activities one could only dream of.

I encourage you, if you are going to take a leap into the unknown, the best way to do it, is to **DO.IT. AFRAID.**

Chamo Chapter Tip

"...when it feels uncomfortable it is a clear indication you are heading in the right direction."

SECTION II

The Colors

The Olympic Rings

The Olympic logo is made up of five rings. Each ring is a different color consisting of blue, yellow, black, green and red. These rings interlock one another and stands as visible brand to one of the most elite form of athletics ever created. The traditional breakdown and meaning behind the interlocking colored rings were to be universally accepting of all nations participating in the games. The number five represents the five continents where athletes travelled from to compete. While the specific colors and a white background have no significant meaning, it is inclusive of one color from every nation's flag. The overall message of the flag, the logo and the interlocking color rings is UNITY!

In August of 2012, I had the privilege of attending the summer Olympics in London. The excitement started the minute my co-worker casually said, "Hey! I am going to visit my family in England next month. Oh and by the way I got tickets to the Olympics, wanna go?" I don't think she finished her sentence before I started looking up flights. Not only was going to the Olympics an item on my ever growing bucket list, but my country (Team Jamaica) was dominating the Track & Field competition and I finally would be there to experience it. What I didn't know was all the wisdom, courage, and enlightenment I would come back with. Talk about a souvenir!

The Olympic Park is like the holy grail of sports and recreation. It is very intricate in design and construction. Besides the fact that the location of the games is decided years in advance, the actual park takes several years to build. One of the most important logistics is the flow of which the athletes can get to practice and compete as well as managing thousands of excited fans, like myself who just want to stand there and breathe the Olympic air.

I have to admit, the minute you step foot in the Olympic park a sense of pride builds up in your chest. After all, this is the upper echelon of sports and you are witnessing records being broken and history being made. Seeing your country's flag and emblems everywhere you turn on every nook and cranny gives you a sense of belonging, a sense of home. The coolest part of the park experience, is at every turn you would run into an athlete and it didn't matter that they represented a different country; they were all celebrities in my eyes.

It was the morning after the closing ceremonies, and I was on an early 6 a.m. flight out of London Heathrow. I was exhausted from adrenaline and excitement that I exerted over the past several days. Typically for long flights, I dress extremely comfortable and on this particular morning, I decided to wear my recently purchased Adidas track suit designed with the Jamaican flag colors and my official 2012 Olympic rings pin on my lapel. The moment I walked into the airport I noticed everyone staring at me. At first I didn't pay it any mind, but the farther I walked to the ticketing counter, the more people stared and then started to whisper. So I did what any normal woman would do, I stopped, pulled out my compact mirror and prepared myself to find something horrendous on my face. After all, it was 6 a.m. in Europe and my brain was still half asleep. Mirror check, nope nothing on my face. I did a quick body look over, nope nothing there either. At this point I am joining the ticket line and getting very annoyed at how rude these people are being. Finally, a woman and her friend walked up to me and asked "Are you part of the Jamaican team? What do you run? How is it training with Usain Bolt, we love him!" Then it hit me, these people think I am athlete! Ha, the perception could not have been more off as I couldn't run up a flight of stairs if my life depended on it. My first thought was "Michelle go along with it and get your 15 minutes of fame" until the realistic thought intercepted with "What if they actually Google you?" Reality won and I proceeded to now let these women know for sure I am no athlete and simply just a fan that came to support. Unfortunately, by this time they motioned for someone to come and take a picture. As the photographer is setting up to take the picture, they both pull a piece of lanyard that's tucked underneath their shirt. I look, then look closer and realize it's a GOLD MEDAL hanging from their necks. Please understand that I had NO clue who either of these women were, but I deduced they had just won the highest medal possible in the Olympics. I stand there, take the picture and then proceed to tell them again that I was not an athlete but they are merely caught up in reviewing the picture. They turn around and say thank you and walk off and I continue on to the ticket line while chuckling to myself. I ask the agent if she knew who they were and she responded the USA Women's Soccer Team (go figure). From that point on, from the check-in counter to the concession stand, I was repeatedly asked if I was an athlete.

Finally, I make it to my window seat and prepare to get some much needed sleep when I hear the flight attendant say "Let's give a round of applause for all our athletes and medalists on this flight!" The entire plane erupts in cheer and applause and the guy sitting next to me turns and says "Congratulations, how far did you get in the trials?" I chuckle again and explain to him that not only am I not an athlete, but that I have been stared at and asked that for the past hour prior to boarding. He then shares with me that he won a Silver Medal in Wrestling and that he couldn't wait to get back to the States to start training for the next Olympic Games.

This is the part of the story where the actual "ah ha" moment happened for me and the point when the concept of this book came about. If you break down the path to make it to the Olympics, it is intimidating yet inspirational at the same time. To think you start off at the lowest possible level by identifying you have athletic abilities somewhere around middle school. By the time you reach high school, you would have a platform to start building on that ability. Then college allows you to learn technique and thereafter you start competing on a professional level. You continue to practice, compete and fight, raising the bar for yourself higher with each competition. You do this so you can ultimately go toe-to-toe and compete with and against the best and ultimately win a medal that classifies you as the most elite and distinguished in your sport field. What an honor it is to be called an "Olympic Medalist".

As this young man continues to converse with me about how grueling training is, I asked him how does he not break down physically. His response was one I remind myself of very often. The body is bound to feel pain once it has been overly exerted. No one, not even an athlete is exempt from that. Rather than focusing on the pain, shift your mental well-being into overdrive. Use your mind sort of like a "backup generator" for your home. Similar to when you have a power loss in your home, your backup generator kicks in to provide temporary power to get you through the power failure. He went on to say that you almost have to train your brain harder than your body because your physical is guaranteed to die on you faster than your brain will. Talk about a power shift!

How many times have you had to start from the lowest level and fight your way through something, losing your main energy source along the way? It is at that point where you take must make that power shift and use your other emergency power pack (mental) to take you across the finish line. Ultimately everything you work towards should be compared to the Olympic gold medal. If you miss achieving your goal the first time, you go back and retrain. Make a major part of that training to be training your brain to kick into high gear – mind over matter. Remember the five colored Olympic rings? Well my rings represent my (Black) physical well-being, (Blue) my mental state, (Yellow) my spirituality, (Red) my determination and (Green) my support system all interlocked to create unity and ultimately get the gold medal!

Once in a BLUE

It was January 1, 2010, at 7 a.m. I was driving with a close friend of mine, accompanying her to take pictures, as she embarked on a crazy adventure. What started as support for her ended up being a life-changing activity for me. As we drove on a desolate highway, we started to see objects in the sky that appeared bigger the closer we got to our destination. It was people falling from the sky! I fully understood that in just a few hours my friend was going to be another one of those tiny objects. Never once did it cross my mind that it would be me also. Yes, on that New Year's Day, I went on my first sky dive.

The color blue wasn't actually the color that was flashing through my eyes and thoughts during this process. In fact, any color that represented fear is what I was seeing. Surely, I thought, I wasn't going to voluntarily jump out of a fully, good functioning plane. To this day, my friend and I still debate that I was peer pressured into this activity. Yet, I on my own will, I ultimately signed the, "THERE IS A POSSIBILITY DEATH MAY OCCUR" portion of the agreement and waiver, so I digress.

We were suited up waving to the camera as we walked to this tiny plane, my friend - smiling, me - blank stare. Externally, you couldn't tell that I was petrified. Internally, I wanted to turn and walk right back into the administration building. The manager of the facility told me that he is pairing me with his most experienced diver, who had about 4,500 dives under his belt. Then he said "Would you believe me if I told you it feels the total opposite of a roller coaster?" I'm not sure why I chose to trust this complete stranger at that moment; he just got my money and signed waiver that his company would not assume any responsibility of my death, but I did.

Fast forward to the inside the plane, I see about 7-8 young men pile in after my friend and me. My tandem jumper tells me that the men are experienced divers who will be practicing a formation. I start to cry, then pray, then both at the same time, repeatedly asking myself "What am I doing?" I then specifically asked my tandem diver – Tim, "Can we jump first so I could avoid seeing or anticipating what will happen next?" I wanted to go first and get it over with.

Without warning Tim starts to prepare us for the jump. I hear harnesses click, straps being tightened, watches being set and stomachs start to sink (well my stomach at least). The door to the airplane flies open, no one says a word and one by one these experience divers jump out of the plane head first. I would blink; they would be sitting in front of me. Then blink again and they would be gone, that quickly. I see my friend move up to the front and then off she went, leaving me and Tim as the last jumpers in the plane. I guess my request to jump first, went out the door with the other jumpers.

I glance down at Tim's altitude watch and I see 14,000 feet. I was scared, to death, almost numb. The emotions that ran through my head were so mixed up I didn't know whether to cry, scream or just be silent. Before I could gather my thoughts and get my bearings together, Tim had pushed us towards the door and out we went backwards. There was no countdown, no ready-set-go, nothing. However, I felt nothing. No nausea, no sinking stomach, no heart palpitations, no asthma attack.

When I opened my eyes, it was like I was floating, through the blue sky. It was such a freeing feeling, pure and light. We did a free fall for about a minute until the parachute was deployed. The remaining 2-3 minutes down was the quietest and most serene environment I have ever experienced.

After that dive, I recognized that my fear was all mental; something that I concocted in my head to help coax my decisions. Sky diving showed me that physically some things may not appear to be as bad as you think. Sometimes you just have to make the jump to see what it could turn out to be. It was also the push for my new beginning. Four months after that dive, I packed up my belongings and moved to Texas to start my new life in a new surrounding with new people. It turned out to be one the best decision I have ever made.

The YELLOW Pages

I decided to use this chapter to talk about the time in my life where the color yellow showed up and how it became instrumental in one of the biggest transitional decisions I could ever make. Remember back in chapter three when I shared my story on relocating to Texas. I was so paranoid of shipping all of my belongings, including my car from New York to Texas because of all the horror stories I have heard, so I decided to drive. I packed all of my things that could fit in my sedan and like the birds, headed south. Please note, I am not one for any long distance driving. I typically prefer an airplane as my mode of long distant transportation. However, my decision to relocate to a foreign place was already in gear, so I tried to remain consistent with my new "Do It Afraid" mantra.

For the first six to eight hours, my drive was going fine. I had a slew of people who called and my Pandora music stations that kept me ample company to last me for weeks! I got to South Carolina and must have driven right into what looked like the apocalypse. It was raining, no, it was torrential raining! No, not even that, it was more like a baby hurricane. It was raining so heavy that even my poor windshield wipers couldn't keep up on the fastest speed.

To my right and there were semis whizzing by me, splashing enough water to fill a pond on my car. I continued driving with hopes that it would clear up in a mile or so. I was wrong; that monsoon continued for about another 45 minutes. It took me 15 minutes just to change lanes! I started getting into panic mode. I simply could not see 10 feet ahead of me much less see through my windshield. My vision was completed blurred. My hands hurt so bad from gripping the steering wheel; I could feel the throbbing in my wrists. Then it happened. I started to cry. I was falling apart at the seams.

I questioned myself through my tears, *"Michelle what are you doing? Why would you leave your safe haven to go somewhere that is unfamiliar? Why did you think driving half way across the country was a good idea? What were you thinking?"* After finally making it over into the right lane I said out loud, "God if I am not supposed to go to Houston, if that's not the next stop on my life journey, show me a sign and I promise I will turn this car around and go back home!" Then it thundered, followed by lightening. For some reason I did not stop driving. I said, "OK God, great way to show me a sign, but am I supposed to turn around because of thunder and lightning, show me another sign?" Needless to say, it kept raining and I kept driving.

My conversation with myself went from, "You're nuts to do this." to "Girl you got this, you're going to make it. Prove it to yourself that it's not a big mistake and if it is, at least you tried." After about an hour of driving in this inclement weather, out of nowhere the rain just stopped and most beautiful rainbow appeared accompanied by the brightest ray of yellow sunshine.

There are so many times in life where you go through a storm and you have no idea when it will end. Your vision will be blurry, skewed and difficult for you to see ahead. Your hands and body may grow weary from fighting and battling your way through the storm. Just know that at the end of every bad day, phase, or situation, I can guarantee that the yellow ray of hope, optimism, clarity and focus will follow. Don't give up when the storm gets rough. Remember although quitting may seem easier than trying, you will miss out on brilliant sunshine, and the sense of accomplishment. Follow it through, see it to the end and smile when you reach the rainbow because you made it.

BLACK Belt

On my visit to Thailand in 2014, I saw the color orange used in such a peculiar way. I travelled to the Kho Phi Phi Islands to go diving. At the time I had been a certified scuba diver for 2 years and had 12 open water dives under my belt. No matter how many times I get on a dive boat, it never fails that my nerves kick in and I get scared. Internally, I am trying to remember all the rules and safety measures for diving and I always seem to draw a blank. After getting geared up, and the moment comes for me to jump off of a perfectly good boat into a not so friendly ocean, fear walks right up and sits next to me. Each time I always try to talk myself out of it. By the time I do jump in, I exert so much energy in breathing, that I use half the air in my tank before I even descend under water. On this particular day on this particular boat, there was a guy named Paul. What Paul didn't know was that he gave me a first class lesson on "Never underestimate your ability!"

When I first saw Paul on the boat, he looked like a normal middle age man in great shape. When Paul started to get suited up, I noticed he was an amputee. Without being rude, I watched him put on his wetsuit, then his tank (which weighs about 40-50 lbs.), his goggles and he kept his fin in his hand. I was a bit concerned because I know how difficult it is for even me, with two legs, to put my fins on when I am sitting on the boat much less once I am already submerged in the water. From the left side of me, I see my dive master walk over to Paul to assist him getting in the water. Paul kindly, yet assertively declined the offer. It was almost as if the dive master was insulting him. Then Paul sat down at the edge of the boat and gracefully bounced in the water and immediately put on his fin. His demeanor was calm, cool and collect and he never once appeared flustered; (talk about physical energy and resilience). I then had to chin check myself. Here is a man who I felt at the time had less ability than me and is proving before my very eyes that you can do anything you put your mind to. That was the first time I didn't have to coach myself to jump in and had a smooth and successful dive. On that day, Paul was a perfect example that you can still fulfill your goals (big or small) despite any shortcomings. Like being a Black Belt in martial arts, it takes tenacity, confidence in your abilities and the hunger to want to succeed. Paul was the real MVP.

The Best Things in Life Are GREEN

I did a quick informal survey and asked 20 random people, "What was the first thing that came to mind when they heard the word green?" Unanimously, they all answered "MONEY". It is amazing how this one color is just about always identified with the U.S. currency. Some say 'money makes the world go round', others say 'more money more problems'. Yet the color green can yield you value that has nothing to do with currency.

Tangible Abundance

vs.

Intangible Abundance

I took a second and questioned my own view of the color green and what stood out to me was what I truly considered abundance. Then I asked myself, "What is it that I truly want to be abundant in?" Surely, I like to live a comfortable lifestyle that allows me to indulge in things of my liking. However, I also value 'time'. How else would I be able to enjoy these indulgences? If I had the choice I would rather have an abundance of time over abundance of wealth any day. While money can buy you just about anything, it cannot buy you time.

Recently, I read an article about a prominent Investment Banking CEO who was worth over $100 million. He travelled the world and could buy literally whatever his heart desired, that was until he received a note from his young daughter. In the note she listed 22 milestones that he had missed in her life such as her first soccer match and first parent-teacher conference. After much debate or rather excuses as to why he was not around for her more often, it hit him that he could never get that time back with her so he resigned from his high profile job.

There was another article about another young girl who wrote a letter in crayon and sent it to her father's job at Google asking for them to give her dad a day off. She noted that he only got Saturdays off and would like him to have more days off to spend time with her. It was her father's birthday, but she also noted that it was summer as to imply that no one should work during the summer (I like the way she thinks!). Not only was her letter received by her father's boss, but he granted him a week of vacation and alternating Wednesdays off.

Much is to be learned from these younger people who clearly see the color green in a whole different perspective. They had no concept of wealth, but understood the value of the time that their parent was missing with them. Without even reading these stories, I have always desire the freedom to live out my passions. The idea of being rich and famous is appetizing to most people, me included. However, I think when you're rich in time, in love, in support, in health, in favor, and in blessings combined, that makes you wealthy in life! It doesn't get any greener than that!

Lady in RED

I have never been a fan of the color red. I had always thought of it as a loud and obnoxious color; however, throughout my career it has served as an integral part of some of my biggest wins to date. Back in chapter one I spoke about having an emotional moment and temporarily shifting in order to get through a particular day to have a successful event. Here is a tip of how the color red could have helped me conquer that day or any intimidating situations in my career and in life.

Having spent most of my career working on Wall Street in Investment Banking, the culture compares to swimming with sharks; only the strongest survive. There is a common theme amongst all who are a part of that world, "Every second equates to a dollar!" Therefore, there is little room for idle time, ad hoc conversations or activities that would deter one away from getting to their bottom line, especially if you have ever worked on the trading floor. Even now, living in Texas, having worked in

Oil/Gas/Energy, time is equivalent to money.

Presenting in front of a group of people has never frightened me. Typically I am usually quite comfortable in front of an audience because I am generally talking about things I am well versed on, like myself (which is always the easiest), career advancement, or simply life experiences. Over the past several years I have had the opportunity to work closely with Senior Level Management including a CEO. Let me set the scene. Picture it – You walk into a boardroom with individuals who have Masters Degrees and PhD's from the top Ivy League business schools to lay a presentation on them. These executives don't get out of bed for deals less than $50 million and here I am walking in to present to them. Fast forward to the Oil/Gas/ Energy industry, I work in now. Those boardrooms are filled with engineers who fundamentally and often times are some of the smartest people in the room. Trust that engaging an engineer, in which I'll have to admit, are pretty sharp in the education and logic department, you better have done your homework, crossed the 'T's, dotted the 'I's, and selected the right punctuation marks because they will NOT miss an error. When faced with these nerve-racking situations and individuals, I try to always invoke the color red in my strategy. I do it as simple as wearing a red blazer or a red piece of clothing. The color red exudes power in an intimidating environment. Not only does the eye tend to dart quickly to the color red, it also intrigues those who are viewing you.

Yes, I'll admit, I am probably not as smart as the engineer or as business savvy as the investment banker, but I am very confident in my ability to present and engage an audience. When you insert red into those types of circumstances, you pull the audience into you. They first are drawn to you by the bold color and question "who is this bold woman?" Then once you have received their undivided attention, you can proceed on delivering a succinct yet impactful presentation. Since time is money, in those situations you have very little time to make a big impact. The power of the red draws your audience in quickly putting the power in your hands to present a concisely and effectively. It eliminates the need to have to win over your audience first.

Ever watched a presidential debate? When you have a spare moment Google "Presidential Debates" images. Take notice to who is wearing the red tie? If not always, at least one candidate will have on a red tie. In all actuality, the tie color has no effect on who has won the debate or the election. However, wearing red does read better on camera. Again your eye tends to dart to the person wearing it first. If you think about it deeper, the person in the red wants their power to come across, even before they know which way the debate will sway. They try to set the tone from the beginning that they are in it to win. It is all about perception. And as we all know, perception can be a powerful persuader.

My red blazer is like my presidential debate tie. It helps me give the perception that I have come to win. There is no reason why anyone should know you are nervous or anxious before presenting or having a conversation. Put on your red blazer as your confidence booster, shift into who you need to become to get your message across and WIN!

A Message from the Author

There was a point in my career where I was given what I thought to be the worst feedback ever. I was told that my writing skills were poor and inadequate.

Not only did those words play on my insecurities, it also fed my ambition and gave birth to my passion. Thank you for reading.

Section III

The Shift

iShift

The small guide to start you on your shifting journey

Shifting Tips

- Don't be scared to shift. It's temporary and doesn't last forever.
- The power in shifting starts with your choice. Choose to win!
- Make shifting a habit. It will come easier when you need it the most.
- Shifting is not to appease others; it's designed for you to get to your desired goal.
- Your shift will look differently from others. Don't compare.
- Others who have a hard time shifting will not understand how you are able to do it; keep shifting all over them anyway. IT WILL STICK!
- The moments where you feel at your optimal low are the optimal moments to take a shift.
- Get infected with the SHIFT and spread it all over the world.
- Words whisper and actions yell. Don't just say it, shift it, believe it, and do it!

- So you shifted and it didn't work, shift differently and try again (there is more than one way to skin a cat).
- You shifted, it worked, you won - Don't forget the lesson that came with it!

What do you have to lose if you shifted for a moment?

_____

_____

_____

_____

_____

_____

_____

_____

_____

_____

_____

_____

_____

_____

_____

_____

_____

_____

_____

_____

_____

_____

When was the last time you did something for the first time? Why has it been so long?

_____
_____
_____
_____
_____
_____
_____
_____
_____
_____
_____
_____
_____
_____
_____
_____
_____
_____
_____

_____

You shifted and it didn't work? What could you have done differently?

_____
_____
_____
_____
_____
_____
_____
_____
_____
_____
_____
_____
_____
_____
_____
_____
_____
_____
_____
_____
_____

_____

_____

_____

_____

_____

_____

_____

_____

_____

_____

_____

_____

_____

_____

_____

_____

_____

_____

_____

_____

_____

_____

_____

_____

How does taking a shift make you feel?

_____
_____
_____
_____
_____
_____
_____
_____
_____
_____
_____
_____
_____
_____
_____
_____
_____
_____
_____
_____
_____

What colors can you use to help you shift?

_____
_____
_____
_____
_____
_____
_____
_____
_____
_____
_____
_____
_____
_____
_____
_____
_____
_____
_____
_____

_____

_____

_____

_____

_____

_____

_____

_____

_____

_____

_____

_____

_____

_____

_____

_____

_____

_____

_____

_____

_____

_____

_____

_____

_____

7 Day Shift Challenge

Day 1 - Have a conversation with a stranger. Be the one to engage them first.

Day 2 - Try something new. Anything!

Day 3 - Try a shifting technique with someone you don't get along with.

Day 4 - Pick a friend and share shifting with them. Create a shifting challenge together for each of you to complete and report back results.

Day 5 - Go to a place where you don't fit in and try shifting there.

Day 6 - Journal what worked and what didn't work. How did shifting make you feel? Remember if you felt uncomfortable and scared, you're on the right track! Keep shifting!

Day 7 - Sign the iShift pledge/ write the iShift pledge and put it somewhere you look at often. Then repeat. Repeat again. Repeat one more time.

Don't be scared SHIFTLESS!

iShift Pledge

I pledge to stop, think and shift in the moment. I want to win and I will win! I am my own Shift Starter!

X_____

Thank you to my AMAZING support system!

Mom, Camille, Andrew, Tavia, Kiesha, Bryan, Errol, my nieces and nephews for being such a solid rock and support in my foundation. I hope I have made you all proud.

Penny, Khalid, Amber, Gloria, Natalie, Erika, Shakira, Sam, Jerry, Jaime, Katy, Angela, Marsha, Aisha, Chaniece, Charlye and Dominique for being my accountability partners and the battery in my back when my confidence was running on low.

Romord and Christy (the "Staple" in my life) for helping to start and finish this project; I'm convinced your timing was one of God's blessings.

Manon, for planting the seed of writing a book in me; and thank you for mentoring in my career!

And to everyone and anyone who has ever sent me a note, a text, a message, gave me a call, thought about me, prayed for me, or cheered me on from afar, I am forever indebted to you.

About the Author

Michelle A. Smith is a self-awareness strategist, who believes that when people tap into their core qualities and characteristics, transformation happens – not only for the individual but, the people around them, and the entire world. As a coach, she supports and challenges individuals to look deep inside, change their color and shift temporarily to reach their desired outcome. Her mission is to offer entertaining and hands on tools and resources that help all people develop the knowledge, skills and confidence to master adapting to changing environments in the 21st century.

Born and raised in the urban city of Flatbush-Brooklyn, New York, through personal experiences, she brings a richly diverse life story to share with people who are ready to transform themselves into the confident and powerful individuals they aspire to be. Over her career, she has given seminars, workshops, speeches and mentored many extraordinary human beings to explore, identify and reach for their goals. She believes it is significant to learn how to temporarily change your external color without changing your internal core of who you are.

A graduate of the State University at Stony Brook, Michelle received a Bachelor's degree in Economics and Business Management. She was certified in etiquette from the Ophelia Devore School of Charm in New York City. Currently, Michelle works as a Human Resources Business Partner for a large Energy company. She is also a member of several professional and nonprofit organizations and was highlighted in the 2012 Who's Who in Black Houston publication. Having been to six continents and over 30 countries across the globe, Michelle enjoys traveling, indulging in various cultures and scuba diving. Her true passion mainly lies in participating in public speaking engagements, workshops and seminars and using any opportunity to create a Shift Starter Movement.

Contact

For more information visit:
www.theshiftstarter.com

For emails, inquiries and requests:
info@theshiftstarter.com

Follow me on:
Facebook – TheShiftStarter
Instagram – TheShiftStarter
Twitter – TheShiftStarter

CPSIA information can be obtained at www.ICGtesting.com
Printed in the USA
LVOW06*0738230315

431484LV00001BA/1/P